How to Make Abstract Paintings

Composition #30. Oil. 22" x 30." HUGH LAIDMAN.

HOW TO MAKE
ABSTRACT
PAINTINGS

BY

HUGH LAIDMAN

A STUDIO BOOK

The Viking Press   NEW YORK   1961

FIRST PUBLISHED IN 1961 BY THE VIKING PRESS, INC.
625 MADISON AVENUE, NEW YORK 22, N.Y.

PUBLISHED SIMULTANEOUSLY IN CANADA BY
THE MACMILLAN COMPANY OF CANADA LIMITED

LIBRARY OF CONGRESS CATALOG CARD NUMBER: 61-6794

PRINTED IN THE U.S.A. BY THE MURRAY PRINTING COMPANY

To my wife

Acknowledgments

To Mrs. Bredemeier of the Carl Bredemeier Gallery (Buffalo, New York) for the beautiful frames; to the Niagara Corrugated Container Company, Division of St. Regis Paper Company, for a full station-wagon load of board; to National Aniline, Division of Allied Chemical Corporation, for flexible foam and technical advice; to Savage Litho, Inc., for paper; to Bob Blair, Larry Griffis, Bruce Horning, Jinx, Bonnie, and Cece for their paintings; and especially to Pete and Jody Hill for their Fridays, Saturdays, and Sundays.

Contents

How to Make Abstract Paintings

Introduction

THIS book explains techniques employed in creating abstract paintings similar to those currently being exhibited in galleries and museums. Few of the techniques employed by the representational painter are discussed, because the aims of the traditionalist and those of the abstract painter differ, and so do many of the materials they use.

It is a great pity that so many explanations of abstract painting offer little more than double-talk. This disturbing tendency, along with the occasional press release or joke concerning paintings hung upside down or stories about amateurs, monkeys, parrots, and practical jokers winning prizes for their work have made the public a little wary of abstract painting. The abstract-art movement is often confusing, more often obscure, but most certainly it is stimulatingly alive. It has a purpose and a place in the modern scheme of things, and should be taken as seriously as any other form of art.

The keynote of modern painting, from the time of Goya, has been that of change. To appreciate modern painting it helps to be aware of the tradition and to realize that no one has really replaced anything, though many have added to it. Today's "action" painters are contributing another step in the history of art. To understand and evaluate just what they are doing, we should approach the subject with an open mind, and, coming still closer to it, paint a few abstract pictures of our own.

Today's abstract painter is influenced by the world around him. He is not a reporter, however. He expresses his emotions and thoughts, and leaves the chronicling to others. He is not illustrating current events; he is creating a new art of his own which is in keeping with the times.

If the patterns of the past continue, the great artists of today have probably not yet been recognized. If we follow further the pattern of the past, the artists most popular at the moment will fade with time. The school of abstract art will become an additional stage in the continuing story of painting. By participation, the neophyte can learn to appreciate this present stage.

Everyone is equipped by nature to receive and assimilate sensory expression. He is sensitive to color, tones, touch, and space relations, and can become a creditable painter, sculptor, architect, or musician. This does not mean that every man is capable of creating fine art and being an artist. Art is the highest level of production in any form. Becoming an artist requires more than following procedures in a book on painting, yet by following procedures one may learn to distinguish a true piece of art from an exercise in paint application.

The line is not always clearly defined between abstract and representational painting, but often the confusion lies in labels and terms. Some consider abstract any deviation from the realistic; others consider abstract only those paintings that have no relation to any objects. While admitting the controversy concerning the merits of realistic versus abstract, traditional versus experimental, and conservative versus radical, this book will concentrate on the "pure" abstract, the experimental, and the radical.

Abstract painting is not reserved for the overly sensitive, the genius. Nor is it reserved for the crackpot. Here we have an art form with such free scope that anyone can participate and greatly profit by the results of his efforts—if not financially, then at least spiritually or therapeutically.

Representational painting, being an image of something, is informational, while pure abstract painting exists not as an image of something but rather as itself. When a person views a representational painting, he is reminded of something he has seen or done or wished to do. When a person views a pure abstraction, he sees the painting as a complete statement, with no reference to anything else. He may get an emotional response from it, he may read things into it, but generally no recognizable object is meant to be depicted.

As a painting becomes less identifiable with natural forms, it becomes more difficult to translate into words, and, as a consequence, more controversial. Frequently when an artist is forced to explain such a work he confuses the issue by using a kind of cultural double-talk. The simple fact remains that pat explanations are not usually possible; and there is no reason why they should be. Examples of abstract art can be enjoyed primarily for pattern, color, texture, and the general atmosphere that each one imparts. Personally I am against weighty psychological interpretations, which often do more harm than good to the cause of the modern artist.

Most paintings used to be images of something. Now, most paintings are images of nothing. A history of "isms," schools, art tempests, and turmoils lies between the two extremes. Many of today's well-known artists have a personal history of art that is almost a capsule of the history of modern art. Just as various schools, styles, and isms have begun with variations on the realistic up to the point where a painting had no recognizable object, so many of the artists have periods in their painting careers where their work was more or less identifiable with images.

For example, a popular artist might have been educated in one of the traditional academies, where he learned to paint realistically from casts and models; then he might have been influenced by experiments in the light of the impressionists and next by the geometry of the cubists. In turn, he might have worked in the action style of the futurists, tried his hand at collage, and, after a violent period as an expressionist, painted pure abstractions. The younger the artist, the more abbreviated the course. And it is possible that the experiences of mature artists have shown where steps in this accelerated art-appreciation course could be eliminated.

An interesting aspect of the history of taste in art is the rigid set of limitations imposed by art buyers on artists. Painters, generally, fall into a number of categories—fine artists, muralists, portraitists, commercial artists, and illustrators—as well as a number of sub-categories. The fine artist has few limitations, and, unfortunately, even fewer prospective buyers. Most muralists are influenced to tell a story realistically, although, once in a while, a relatively abstract mural is commissioned—or accepted—usually from one of the dozen best-established abstractionists. The commercial artist has the most affluent group of prospective buyers, although he may have to be content with a style of work not more recent than that of the post-impressionist school. The portraitist has a more or less unlimited group of prospective purchasers. The artists who sell to industry directly are, in most cases, fine artists willing to sacrifice something to live and able to carry their expressions in paint very close to abstraction.

This is best explained through the eyes of an advertising man. It is generally assumed that the leaders of industry are aware of and receptive to new ideas that will not materially hurt their interests. Possibly, if they were not aware, they would be reluctant to admit it. *Fortune* magazine, whose editorials are aimed at executives, will go almost abstract in its approach to illustration, being careful to balance this with photographs of almost unbelievable clarity and detail. *Holiday* magazine, which appeals to a much larger group including part of *Fortune's* audience, appeals to people who are intending, or would like, to travel. The advertiser presupposes an amount of culture and wealth—not that they are inseparable —and editorially may use a slightly abstract approach. The *Saturday Evening Post,* on the other hand, having the most inclusive audience of the three, is limited to that which is realistic, photographic or, if distorted, only in the tradition of the cartoon. This does not restrain the magazine from printing work from the wildest schools of abstract painting. These illustrations, however, are always in the nature of a report on the subject, not an editorial component of the magazine. It is still considered radical for the *Saturday Evening Post* to reproduce on its cover a portrait in other than the Norman Rockwell tradition. For art directors, an acceptable safety valve from the continual stream of realism is the cartoon. There seems to be no inherent danger to circulation in this minor field of abstraction.

It is not to be inferred that a painting becomes better as it becomes more abstract. Abstraction is no substitute for quality. One of the reasons that more abstract paintings fill today's shows, aside from the obvious one that more of them are being submitted, is that it is relatively easy to hide mediocrity in an "abstract." Generally, it is more difficult to hide inability in a realistic painting. In this respect, realistic painting is a bit like playing the violin; it is sometimes difficult to distinguish the genius from the expert, but there is never any doubt about the amateur.

Quantities of books have been written on how to paint. Most of these have dealt with the naturalistic style. One reason given for this is that one must learn to draw realistically before one can distort effectively. The academies of old went overboard on this theory and thereby often succeeded in boring to distraction otherwise good prospective artists. It is possible that some of the more advanced schools today have swung too far to the other extreme. In painting, even the accidental must be controlled and in some cases made to speak louder than the preconceived. As we get into the experiments on the following pages, we will see how that seemingly contradictory statement becomes a fact.

Before we learn to draw in the traditional manner, we are inherently able to recognize good design from bad, harmony from disharmony. If the teaching process dulls that perception, we have lost rather than gained in "learning to draw." It would seem better to stimulate the perceptive qualities of the individual first, and then learn the tools of the trade; better to take a variety of colorful shapes and arrange them in pleasing designs than to spend hours with a piece of charcoal over a cold plaster cast.

Occasionally it is worth while to return to the world of strict realism. Some very fine abstractionists paint an almost photographic canvas from time to time. This serves as a control on the experimental and radical work. Artists usually notice that successive realistic paintings are the better for their experience in the abstract.

Professional artists generally paint with the thought of showing their work in a gallery, of selling it, or possibly of having the work find its way into an important collection. Amateurs may have the same aims, but these are not necessary for the rewards of painting. There is a great deal of enjoyment just in doing—more especially if the doing is exciting in method. There are innumerable walls that beg for framed paintings. A painting does not need to win a prize or even to be accepted in a show to add something to a home.

Aside from easel paintings, abstract techniques lend themselves to murals, stage sets, ceramic design, and practically any stable surface. The rewards are many—first the doing, then the viewing, and then, as you continue to paint, the reviewing of your current work in relation to your past paintings.

The methods outlined in the next pages will help you create these abstracts.

The conscious appreciation of abstract paintings will be accelerated by exposure to good paintings in exhibitions and galleries only if you have some knowledge of the aims and

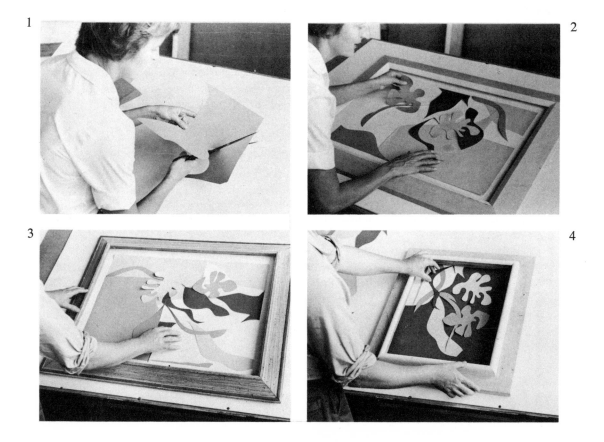

works of the artists. If you have painted a few, however ineptly, you will be even closer to an understanding. The opponents of abstract art refer to this process as "brain-washing" and usually refuse to enter into the process. This is an unfortunate and limited view of painting and, like most narrow views, hurts the viewer as much as anyone else. I am suggesting that you risk being "brain-washed"—paint a few abstracts and study more of them. Paint one full of wild slashing strokes and compare your result with a similar painting in a gallery. In the process you may recognize your painting's inadequacies; you may appreciate more fully the effort of the artist in the gallery painting; you may even see weak passages in his painting. You will certainly be closer to understanding abstract painting.

There is no suggestion here that you imitate the work of others. Attempts at imitating, at best, can only flatter the original. Your best things will be those in which your own ideas and thoughts and feelings appear in paint. In this book we are merely showing a variety of painting methods and do not suggest for a moment that the results will be immediately snapped up by scouts from some museum of modern art. Yet, who knows?

It is a good idea at first to follow procedures step by step, but your work will assume real value only when you have struck out on your own. Most of the steps followed in making the paintings in this book take minimum time for completion. This is to get into the business of producing paintings as quickly and fully as possible. An abstract painter, like anyone else, profits from experience. You will be most exceptional if your first attempts are not somewhat restrained. Only by making one painting after another do most people relax, cast off their inhibitions, and start painting with real pleasure and confidence.

With abstract painting it is not always love at first sight. On the other hand most people, without realizing it, long before any formal exposure to abstract painting, have accepted much that is part of the entire abstract painting school. The pages of our magazines and newspapers are crammed with abstract patterns of type and illustrations. Television commercials and programs have all degrees of abstract pattern. When the art directors have done a good job the viewer knows it, although he may not be aware that he has seen abstract design principles in action.

Artists of all ages employed abstract designs. Every art movement discovers one or two ancient or primitive art forms and, after being influenced to some extent, translates these forms into new discoveries. Any moment someone will discover the unlimited abstract pattern in the Mitla ruins.

Studio

AMONG the assortment of painting techniques shown in this book are a few "action" paintings. Action painting is not a tidy occupation. Chances are you will splatter your clothes, the floor, maybe even the walls and the ceiling; but it is worth it. You will need space and light. North light is the best but is not absolutely necessary. The advantage of north light is its constancy without the disturbing rays of the direct sun. If you were painting from objects and needed constant lights and shadows, as does the painter of naturalistic pictures, north light would be necessary.

The area you make into a studio can be any large room, the attic, the garage, the barn, or the back yard. Barns are ideal because of their size and the fact that they are usually made without large windows, so that the artist-renovator has a choice of window size and light direction. There is also the obvious fact that no one really cares too much if paint drips in a barn. If you are worried about dripping paint on the floor, your concern may show in the painting. Of course, there is nothing to prevent you from protecting the floors with thick layers of newspaper and guarding the walls in like manner. In any event, when painting begins you must be prepared to let yourself go.

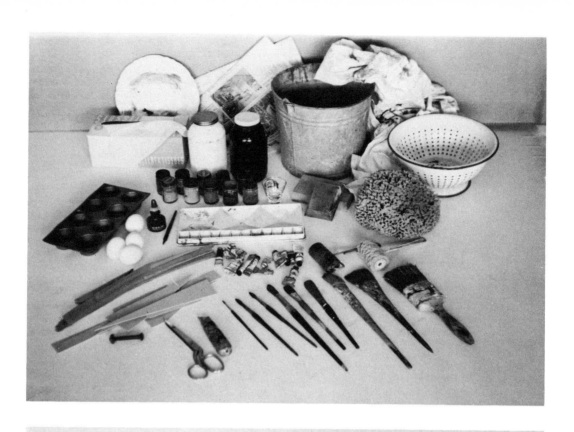

Materials

THE supplies and tools of the abstract painter are inexpensive and easily available. Aside from the traditional tube paints, palette, easel, and brushes, the abstract painter often employs "non-art" materials: corrugated cardboard, building board, burlap, house paint, tinting colors usually used by decorators to produce custom colors for walls, lacquers, alkyd-base paint, automobile enamels, dyes, and plaster. He may use paper picnic plates or muffin tins for palettes, as well as spatulas, knives, colanders, screening, shingles, and any other objects that come in handy as tools.

In making the paintings on the following pages, left-over house paint that otherwise would have hardened on the cellar shelves was used. Nothing can be lost by experimenting with similar "left-overs" if you happen to have them on hand. Their value is in the using of them, in giving the artist an opportunity to throw caution to the winds and throw paint at the canvas. Instead of making a large initial investment, learn how to use left-over or inexpensive paints first. Buy better, more permanent materials later. In the water-color section of the book a set of poster colors (including black and white) was used, and a selection of tubes of fine water colors, a selection of sponges (natural and urethane), rags, blotters, facial tissues, a number of fresh eggs, India ink and pen, newspaper, wrapping paper, seventy-pound water-color paper, printing paper, white corrugated cardboard, a cutting knife, scissors, small rollers, a handy supply of fresh water, and a selection of fairly good brushes (later used as oil brushes). Additional equipment included chisel-point camel-hair sign-painter brushes ranging in width from ½ to 2½ inches, and pointed camel-hair water-color brushes, sizes 4, 6, and 12. These were good brushes. The best brushes are recommended even at the start. Occasionally inferior brushes come in handy, but the poor quality is often too limiting. This is true for water colors more than for oils.

In the oil section of the book, materials included cans of liquid decorator colors, house paint, enamel, and lacquer, tube oil paints, fine artist powder paint, sun-thickened oil, Venice turpentine, and also cheaper, less permanent turpentine and linseed oil (this darkens with time and should be used in work where permanence is no object). Equipment included paint rollers, house-paint brushes from 1 to 4 inches wide, in addition to the good brushes used in water-color work, and (as applicators) palette knives, sticks, spoons, sponges, and rags.

Many surfaces were used for the paintings—canvas, paper, plywood, untempered Masonite, Homosote, plaster board, cardboard, building paper, and a folding screen. Canvas stretched over a frame is the traditional surface for oil painting; it is also the most practical for very large paintings. Unsized canvas can be prepared by first stretching the canvas and then applying a gesso ground. This is a commercially available combination of dry glue, titanium oxide, and gypsum to which you add water and apply as directed on the container. For less permanent work, any of the flat alkyd paints may be rolled over the stretched canvas surface. Many of the ordinary "rubber base" paints make a good surface for either oil or poster colors. Canvas may be bought already sized, in widths up to fourteen feet. It is best to use either all-linen or all-cotton canvas. In these experiments, the least expensive grade of cotton duck was used. Also on hand for these projects were a supply of empty cans, various sizes of cardboard, egg yolks, a screw driver, a stapling gun, shingles, sand, and colored paper. Almost any small object may be found useful as a tool for achieving some interesting effect.

Composition #10. Water color. 20" x 30." HUGH LAIDMAN.

Water Color

IT IS customary today for painters to specialize in either water color or oil. There have been other painting mediums, such as tempera, and some artists have used a mixture of mediums on the same surface. In the interests of availability, our first experiments in abstract painting will be with a type of water color referred to as poster color, erroneously termed tempera, and often referred to by experts as gouache or opaque water color.

Water-colorists traditionally fall into three categories. There are purists, who do not use white or black or anything other than what is broadly referred to as transparent water color. There are those who use white and opaque colors timidly. Then, there are those who just don't care, and pile one type over another with abandon. For the time being, we'll be the third type—a quite practical choice, since transparent colors are expensive, and for this reason tend to restrain many would-be water-colorists.

First we will use the cheapest show-card colors, then graduate to better designers' colors, and eventually use fine water colors. Good water-color paper is expensive, but rough #65 cover stock, available at a paper-supply house, is good enough for the first experiments and will prove economical.

In your first few paintings you cannot expect to have much control over the design. Use your natural talent and taste, and simply let yourself go. If you have a definite shape and color in mind, be prepared to try out a number of variations with the prescribed techniques. In this type of painting the element of accident should be utilized, plus some known facts about the quality of poster-color paints.

21

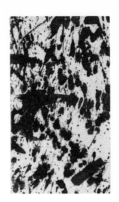

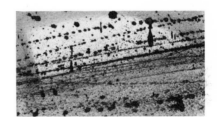

7. Drip and flick
more paint onto
your painting.

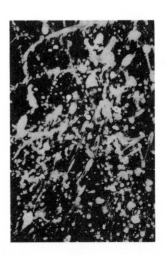

18

Rules and formulas when applied to painting usually fall flat, but here is one that sometimes helps.

Assume that all tones go from black to white. The halftone in the scale would then be a medium gray or about a 50-per-cent gray. In the tone scale shown below *A* would be approximately an 85-per-cent gray and *F* a 15-per-cent gray.

Illustrations *a* and *b,* both roughly following the basic tonal pattern of some well-known old masters, are 85-per-cent gray and 15-per-cent light. The 85-per-cent area has tones from black to 75-per-cent gray whereas the 15-per-cent portion of light has tones from white to about 20-per-cent gray. If we carry this a bit farther and have all the darkest darks in the light area become the lightest lights in the dark area, we simplify the basic design.

In illustration *c,* the same principle has been used in reverse, with the 85-per-cent area light and the 15-per-cent area dark. For emphasis, the darkest dark in the picture is placed near the lightest light and we quickly have a center of interest. In a portrait this would invariably be the facial features, most likely the eyes.

The degree of brilliance of color, apparent design action, texture, and other factors will of course affect the 85-per-cent–15-per-cent theory, but it still remains a good starting point and sometimes even an adequate clue to faulty design.

a

b

c

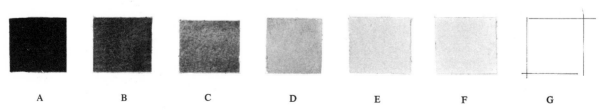

| A | B | C | D | E | F | G |

1. Draw a series of more or less straight lines in charcoal on canvas. You can use brush and a mixture of turpentine and black paint or pencil.

2. Dip black paint from the can with a large putty knife. Apply the paint directly to the canvas. A piece of stiff cardboard is a good substitute for the putty knife.

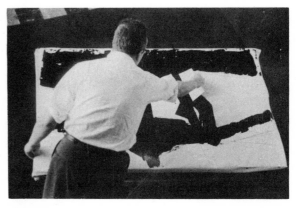

3. Smear the black paint within the general outline of the charcoal sketch.

4. Use a large cardboard as a trowel to define edges and change shapes within the black paint pattern.

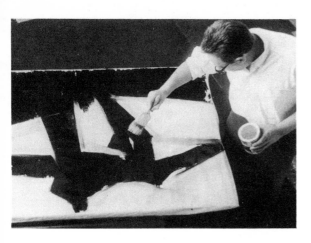

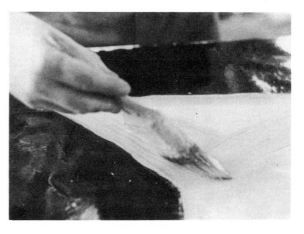

5. Dip an old house-painter brush in white paint and with slashing strokes cover the remaining white canvas.

6. At times some of the wet black paint will be picked up and, as the process of slashing with the brush continues, streaks of gray will become part of the design.

7. With another cardboard trowel scrape the surface to drag the black into the white and the white into the black. As an accent dip the cardboard edge in black and use it to give linear effects in the over-all pattern.

19

2. Place ¾-inch masking tape over the chalk lines.

This is a mechanical approach to a geometric design. This is not action painting, but rather an exercise in tidy paint application.

We've used Masonite (untempered) because tape may be removed from it without damage to the surface. A rigid surface of this kind has the advantage of affording easier control of geometric design. You can substitute tightly stretched canvas, plywood, good illustration board, or high-quality paper.

On this painting we used wall paint, a few scraps of blue, yellow, and red paper, a yardstick and chalk, a house-painter brush along with sign-painter brushes, and masking tape.

Here are a few possible patterns using the tape-design approach.

3. Paint the surface white. Allow it to dry and apply two additional coats of white paint. You can apply this white paint with a roller or a putty knife or a palette knife; either method lends texture to the finished painting.

1. Divide the smooth surface of the Masonite into a pattern of rectangles. Use chalk and a yardstick. Make a number of designs until you have a pleasing composition.

4. Allow the paint to dry and remove the tape.

5. Cut a number of blue, yellow, and red paper rectangles the size of some of the shapes outlined by the masking tape. Experiment with placement of these shapes until you arrive at a design that seems right to you.

6. Once you have determined by the paper experiment the arrangement you wish in the finished painting, fill these areas with the chosen color paint. (This "pin-up" method is a simple way of eliminating time-consuming painting and repainting.)

7. Allow the painted areas to dry. Paint with black the lines left when the tape was removed. If you have run over onto these unpainted lines with the colors, the final black lines will hide the ragged edges. A simple method of painting a straight line is to use a straightedge and pointed brush.

20

In these paintings we started by pouring a good amount of turpentine on a sheet of paper. Then we poured a selection of colors onto this surface and proceeded to rub it to attain a fairly even tone.

1. On paper, wet with turpentine, pour some liquid bla◄ and a few drops of red.

4. On a second sheet of turpentine-soaked paper, apply a mixture of white and flame red. Paint with long, even strokes until the surface is an even tone.

5. With a smaller brush dipped in black and flame r◄ paint a couple of stripes along one edge of the paper.

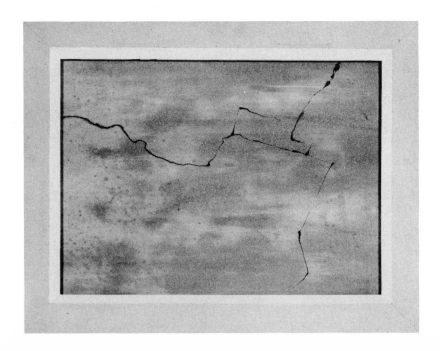

Scrub the surface with a cloth until it becomes an ~~eresting~~ all-over tone.

3. With a screwdriver dipped in black, describe a limited number of lines. See result at bottom of page 66.

On a third sheet of paper, moistened with turpentine, ~~int~~ a mixture of black, flame red, and white. Wipe the ~~ture~~ off with a rag to get a blended surface.

7. Drip a thin line of white over this surface in an erratic pattern. Drip black onto this line in a few spots. Smear the line with your fingers for the result shown below.

21

Cece, the artist in this series, was given a few cans of house paint, each with a little cardboard stick. Since each color had its own applicator, there was little chance of one color's being accidentally mixed with the next. Cece was asked to make shapes she liked, in colors she liked. She took it from there.

1. With a cardboard stick about the length of a big pencil, narrow at one end and wider at the other, apply an interesting area of muted yellow to a prepared painting surface. Mix the yellow with white to cut its intensity.

4. Stand back from your painting and appraise what you have done so far. Turn the painting upside down and look at it as a horizontal painting. Look at it in a mirror.

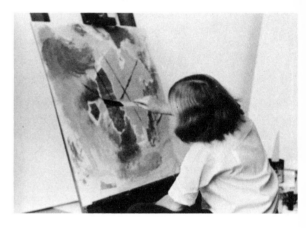

5. Dab accents of black and red next to portions you wish to make important.

6. Frame the painting and make final alterations and improvements.

2. To get a smooth surface with a bit of texture, drag the brush first in one direction, then the other.

3. With a lighter tone of an analogous color, paint the remaining area.

6. Use a clean, dry brush to blend this new dark edge carefully with the first areas. This brush will pick up the paint of lighter areas. Wipe it on rags as you proceed.

7. This could be the finished painting.

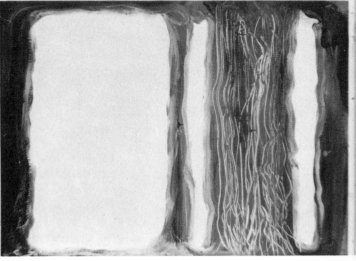

10. With the back of your fingernails describe a pattern in the dark areas.

35

1. Paint the canvas with a thin mixture of ocher and yellow paint and turpentine and oil.

This is a transparent method of painting in oil, similar to methods used for transparent as opposed to opaque water colors. Paint was thinned with oil and turpentine. Sure, crisp strokes were used. The canvas was the one stretched in the series on pages 112 and 113.

2. Wipe the canvas until it has an even tone of color. It will remain slightly damp.

3. Make sharp, quick strokes with the fine edge of a chisel brush. These lines were chartreuse, deep yellow-green, and brownish green.

4. Paint two or three areas of deep brown and one of bright green.

5. While this is still wet, paint a series of almost black-brown and light yellow lines over the last strokes, using a water-color brush. Alternate deep colors and light colors. Here a yardstick is used as a straightedge.

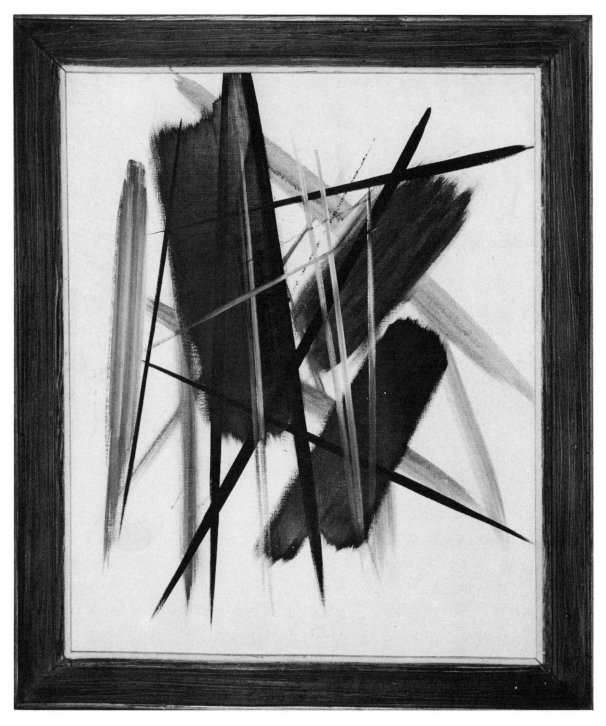

97

36

1. Stretch a very large unsized canvas to a frame and paint it with a basic light tone as a ground. With a 1½ inch brush in one hand and a can of liquid white paint in the other, slash at the canvas, bringing the brush directly from can to the canvas.

The big painting surface is ideal for exercising complete freedom and action in technique. No matter how much time may elapse between the actual start and finish, the work on the painting itself is always done in a frenzy of speed and action. The moment the artist lets up and starts to "tickle" a section, this passage in the painting becomes noticeable for its "worked-over" appearance. This does not mean that this much area must be covered with paint in so many minutes. You may, and probably will, come back again and again to add, change, and take away sections.

4. Stand back and snap the brush onto the canvas to slash areas of light blue, yellow, white, and black until the canvas is full of action. This will be true in almost a literal sense, since the paint will actually be running.

2. Switch to a can of black paint and another brush, and once again sling paint at the canvas.

3. Slap brilliant red onto the canvas with a smaller brush.

5. With tubes of oil color, squeeze paint directly onto the canvas as accents.

6. With brush, hands, the tube swing thinner lines and splatters to bring out the larger areas.

(Continued)

7. After this stage the painting can be modified and, sometime in the future, signed and varnished. This painting will need no frame, because the thickness of the stretcher on which it is mounted serves to give it the necessary effect.

Other Methods and Materials

Two favorite remarks made by first viewers of action paintings are "I could do better with my feet" and "It looks as though a child did it."

On the "If you can't beat 'em, join 'em" theory, a small child was given a few jars of paint and a working area, and was allowed to dance around.

The child loved it, of course, but soon started to direct her feet and the paint. The result (shown in the three photos below)—nothing too striking, although a certain amount of apparent freedom is evident. I doubt that many of us "could do better with our feet."

Three little girls were asked to pick their two favorite colors, then to apply the paint along with any amounts of black and white they wished.

The result was a delightful composition in brilliant, amazing color harmony. We all have an innate feeling for design and color until we are "brainwashed" by rules and fears.

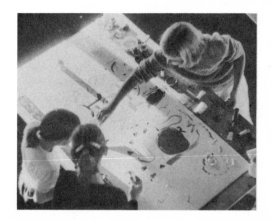

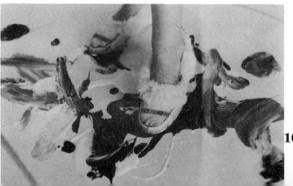

This book has shown mainly oil and water-color methods, but abstract painting lends itself to a great variety of other materials. Lacquers and casein paints have an equal number of possibilities. Varicolored gravel, embedded in thick paint, may be used to give interesting texture and pattern. Broken bits of colored glass, glued or painted onto a surface, producing striking effects. Fiberglas, Celastic, and papier-mâché can also be used in collages with good results, and so can such old standbys as wallpaper, bark, sand, and sandpaper.

Sometimes a collage with objects of relative thickness is pleasing, or, at the very least, startling. Bits of wood, painted or unpainted, shavings, and even mixtures of sawdust are occasionally used. A shingle collage was made as follows.

An arrangement of variously shaped shingles was made on a base of Masonite.

Some of the shingles were painted.

All the shingles were tacked onto the Masonite in pre-arranged locations.

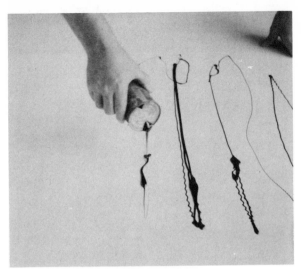

It is possible to make interesting linear effects by pouring tar. Here is the beginning of such an experiment.

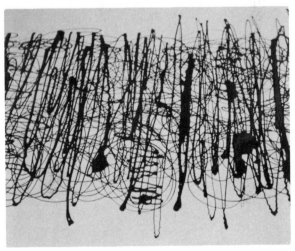

Here is one of the final stages, using tar.

Tar is good only as an exercise, since it never dries properly and is difficult to handle. You can get a similar effect with more permanence and less mess by mixing paint, sun-thickened linseed oil, and turpentine to the consistency of heavy cream.

Using a broom or a scrub brush to pat paint on a surface will give a rather coarse stipple effect.

Chisel out a design in plywood to get a ragged effect about one layer deep. (Continue the steps shown below.)

Try laying chicken wire on a board and patting paint over it. Remove wire to leave a design in high relief.

Rub a tone of paint over the unchiseled portions of plywood.

A linoleum-paste spreader can be used to drag paint into fascinating patterns.

Pour paint into the low areas. Here metallic paint was used.

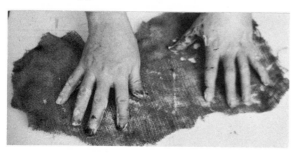

Cloth, parts of rugs, even floor tiles can be pressed into thick coatings of paint to make patterns.

Rub the entire area again, to clean the drips around the newly painted areas.

Press paint through a window screen or press a bit of screen onto tacky paint.

Ideas For Painting

Each artist has his personal approach to creating paintings. This may be anything from pure inspiration, a spontaneous feeling within him, to an idea that he has carefully worked out in his mind beforehand. Whatever the approach may be, that is the beginning of a painting. Even the most creative person is sometimes devoid of ideas. For these times, which professionals usually call "dry periods," here are a few ways to stimulate ideas.

Make some doodles in color, using Magic Markers, pastel crayon, colored ink, or water color, and see what designs suggest themselves for further development. Or spatter ink, smear paint, or arrange several small objects of different shapes, colors, and textures and make a collage.

105

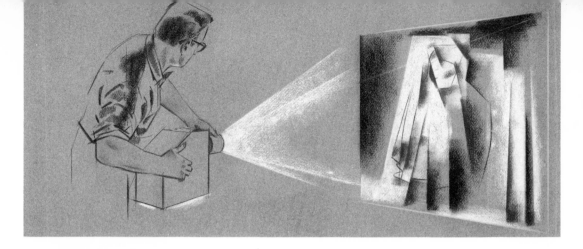

If you have a magic lantern or can borrow one, project your doodles onto a much larger flat surface. With magnification they assume new importance; the change of scale seems to lend authority. This method eliminates the more arduous task of enlarging a small sketch into a large-scale experimental painting. Adjustments can be made.

Project color transparencies, holding the screen at various angles to get distorted effects. If you put the image out of focus you will get still other effects. Make quick color notes following the design of the projection.

Even for abstract painting, the best source of inspiration is usually landscape or the human figure.

Selecting Parts of a Painting

You will often observe artists appraising parts of paintings (usually those of other artists) by holding up their hands and making a frame that sections off some detail. This selection process is a good method to exercise judgment in matters of composition. Sometimes a painting in its entirety has a few poor sections, or just too many sections. By eliminating part of such a painting, you can arrive at a much better finished product—and possibly more than one. The same "framing" process is, of course, also used when studying details of landscapes outdoors or any other real-life subject.

To speed up the selection process, you can make two large "L" shapes of cardboard and use these for your framing of details. The four illustrations below show how a number of possible paintings can be made from a single large one. This large drip painting (five feet square) and the paintings on the next four pages are part of a number made to decorate a country club. They were flashy, lively things with little content but lots of good accidental passages.

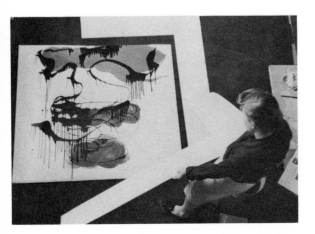 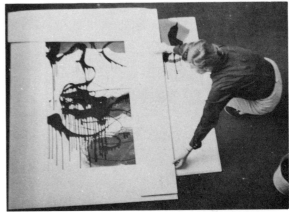

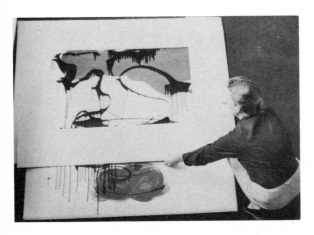 

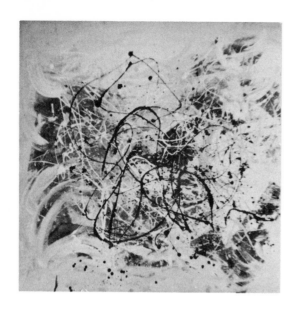

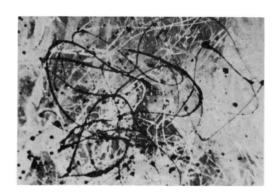

Four details taken from the painting at top left. Each
in itself could be a separate painting.

108

Six details from the painting at top left.

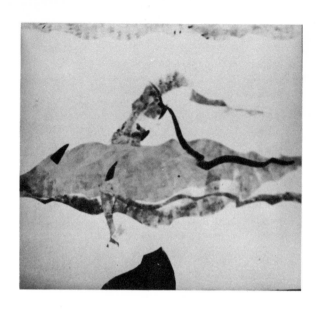

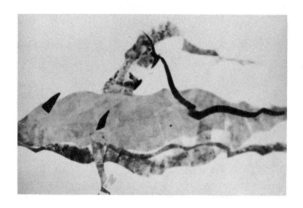

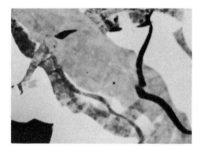

Six details from the painting at top left.

Final example showing how a single painting
can be divided to make separate compositions.

Stretching a Canvas

1. Join the ends of the canvas stretcher pieces as tightly as you can. This can usually be done without the aid of a hammer. The pieces of bought stretchers are well machined, and when joined form a fairly accurate square or rectangle.

2. Check the right angles of the stretcher frame with a triangle. Lay the frame on the canvas. Allow the thickness of the frame all around and mark the frame to the size needed. Here the two sides were used as a straightedge to scribe the canvas with a pencil.

3. Cut the canvas to the size required.

Wooden canvas stretchers come in ready-made sizes up to five feet. Even at five feet, they need a bit of bracing. Most stretchers larger than five feet can be made simply and inexpensively with lumber from the local mill. Study the construction of a ready-made stretcher, then cut four lengths of wood to the size you want.

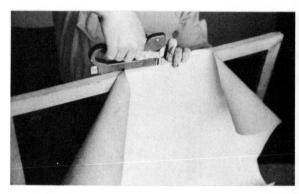

4. Tack the canvas onto the center of one side of the frame.

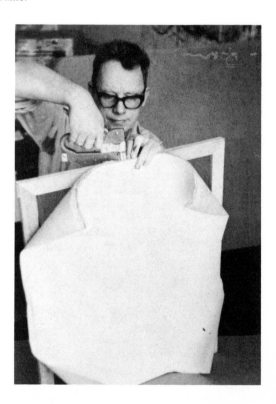

5. Tack the canvas onto the center of the opposite side of the frame. Stretch the canvas fairly taut. This is the easiest time to stretch it, but also the time when it needs the least tightening.

112